★ ★ **Ulysses S.** ★ ★

GRANT

BreAnn Rumsch

Big Buddy Books

An Imprint of Abdo Publishing
abdopublishing.com

abdopublishing.com

Published by Abdo Publishing, a division of ABDO, PO Box 398166, Minneapolis, Minnesota 55439. Copyright © 2017 by Abdo Consulting Group, Inc. International copyrights reserved in all countries. No part of this book may be reproduced in any form without written permission from the publisher. Big Buddy Books™ is a trademark and logo of Abdo Publishing.

Printed in the United States of America, North Mankato, Minnesota
062016
092016

Design: Sarah DeYoung, Mighty Media, Inc.
Production: Mighty Media, Inc.
Editor: Rebecca Felix
Cover Photograph: Getty Images
Interior Photographs: Alamy (pp. 9, 29); AP Images (p. 21); Corbis (pp. 5, 6, 7, 11); Library of Congress (pp. 13, 15, 19, 25, 27); National Archives (p. 23); North Wind (pp. 7, 17)

Cataloging-in-Publication Data

Names: Rumsch, BreAnn, author.
Title: Ulysses S. Grant / by BreAnn Rumsch.
Description: Minneapolis, MN : Abdo Publishing, [2017] | Series: United States
        presidents | Includes bibliographical references and index.
Identifiers: LCCN 2015957468 | ISBN 9781680780956 (lib. bdg.) |
        ISBN 9781680775150 (ebook)
Subjects: LCSH: Grant, Ulysses S. (Ulysses Simpson), 1822-1885--Juvenile
        literature. | Presidents--United States--Biography--Juvenile literature. |
        United States--Politics and government--1868-1877--Juvenile literature.
Classification: DDC 973.8/2092 [B]--dc23
LC record available at http://lccn.loc.gov/2015957468

Contents

Ulysses S. Grant 4

Timeline 6

Young Lyss 8

West Point 10

A Brave Soldier 12

Family Man 14

Civil War Hero 16

President Grant 22

Around the World 26

Office of the President 30

Presidents and Their Terms 34

Glossary 38

Websites 39

Index 40

Ulysses S. Grant

Ulysses S. Grant was the eighteenth US president. Before his presidency, Grant served in the US Army. As president, Grant fought for the Fifteenth **Amendment**.

In 1872, Grant was reelected. He faced problems in his second term. During this time, there were many **scandals** in his party.

Grant tried his best to lead the country. Still, his **reputation** as president suffered. However, Grant will always be remembered as a military hero.

Timeline

1822
On April 27, Hiram Ulysses Grant was born in Point Pleasant, Ohio.

1843
Grant finished school at the US Military Academy at West Point.

1861
The **American Civil War** began on April 12.

1864
Grant was promoted to lieutenant general of all the **Union** armies.

1869

On March 4, Grant became the eighteenth US president.

1872

Grant was elected to a second term as president.

1865

The **American Civil War** ended.

1885

Ulysses S. Grant died on July 23.

Young Lyss

Hiram Ulysses Grant was born on April 27, 1822, in Point Pleasant, Ohio. Everyone called him Lyss. He was the oldest of six children. When Lyss was one year old, his family moved to a farm in Georgetown, Ohio. Around age five, Lyss began his education.

★ FAST FACTS ★

Born: April 27, 1822

Wife: Julia Dent (1826–1902)

Children: four

Political Party: Republican

Age at Inauguration: 46

Years Served: 1869–1877

Vice Presidents: Schuyler Colfax, Henry Wilson

Died: July 23, 1885, age 63

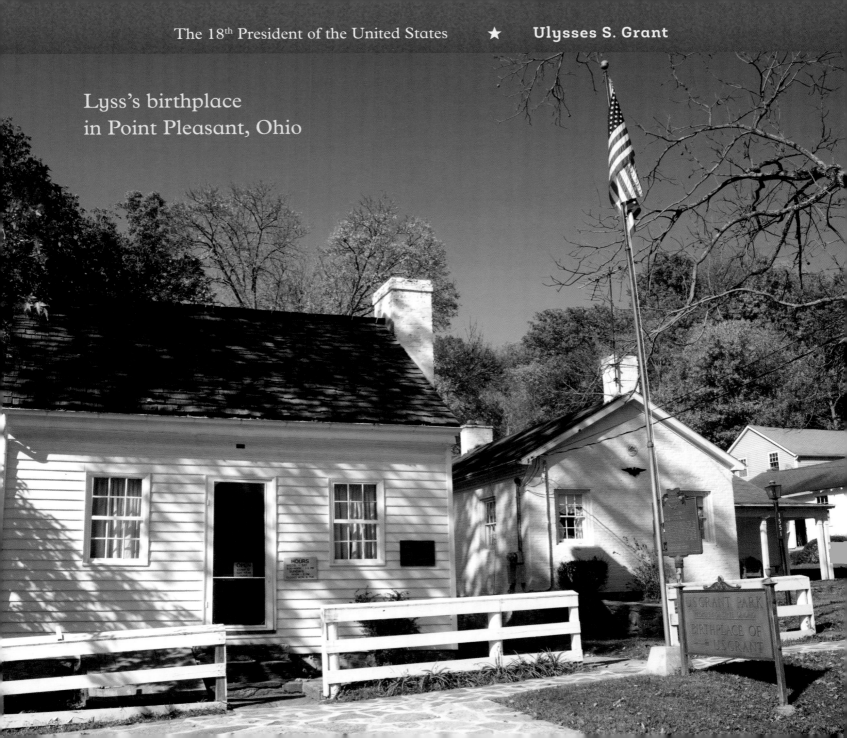

Lyss's birthplace
in Point Pleasant, Ohio

West Point

In 1838, Grant attended the Presbyterian **Academy** near Georgetown. He was then accepted to the US Military Academy at West Point. Grant's father helped him get in.

In 1839, Grant started school at West Point. School officials thought his name was Ulysses Simpson Grant. From then on, he went by Ulysses S. Grant.

Grant finished school at West Point in 1843. He then became a **brevet** second lieutenant. He was stationed near Saint Louis, Missouri.

Grant was an average student. He finished in the middle of his class at West Point.

A Brave Soldier

While in Missouri, Grant met Julia Dent. The two decided to get married. But the army sent Grant to Mexico before they could.

The **Mexican-American War** began in 1846. Mexico did not like that the United States had **annexed** Texas. The two countries also disagreed about the Texas-Mexico border.

During the war, Grant was recognized for his bravery. The United States won the war in 1848. By then, Grant had become a **brevet** captain.

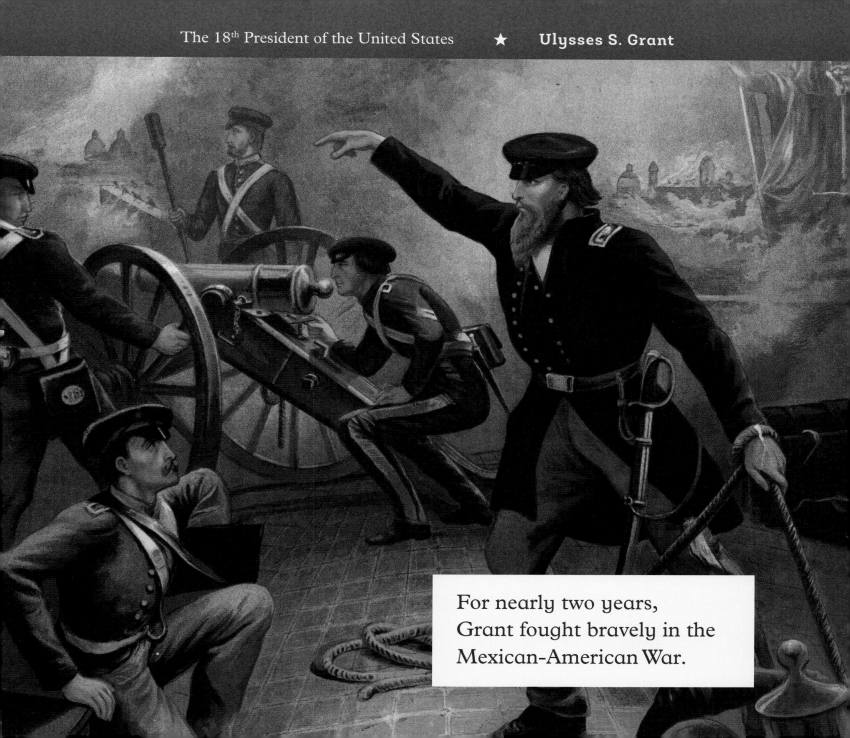

For nearly two years,
Grant fought bravely in the
Mexican-American War.

Family Man

After the **Mexican-American War**, Grant returned to Missouri. There, he married Julia. The Grants went on to have four children.

In 1852, the army sent Grant to the Pacific Coast. But he missed his family. So, in 1854, Grant quit the army and returned home.

Back in Missouri, Grant tried farming. He then worked in **real estate**. But he was not suited to either job. So, in 1860, the Grants moved to Galena, Illinois. There, Grant worked in his father's leather shop.

The Grants had three sons and one daughter.

Civil War Hero

At this time, Americans disagreed about slavery. Northerners wanted to end the practice. Southerners wanted to allow it.

Beginning in 1860, several Southern states left the United States. They formed the **Confederate States of America**. On April 12, 1861, the **American Civil War** began.

The Northern states were known as the **Union**. Grant trained Union soldiers. He was soon put in command of all the troops of southeast Missouri.

Grant's troops won the Battle of Fort Donelson in February 1862. This win made Grant famous.

In April 1862, Grant won the Battle of Shiloh in Tennessee. But thousands of **Union** soldiers were killed, wounded, or missing. The heavy losses hurt Grant's **reputation**.

In November 1863, Grant rescued Union troops that were surrounded by **Confederates** in Chattanooga, Tennessee. This win added to Grant's fame. In March 1864, he became lieutenant general of all Union armies.

Throughout 1864, Grant led Union troops into many bloody battles. People began calling him "Grant the Butcher." Still, Grant kept leading Union troops.

Grant at Cold Harbor, where 6,000 Union soldiers died in battle

In June 1864, Grant led **Union** soldiers to Petersburg, Virginia. The fighting there lasted nearly a year. On April 9, 1865, **Confederate** General Robert E. Lee **surrendered** to Grant. The **American Civil War** was over.

In August 1867, Grant served as President Andrew Johnson's **secretary of war** for a short time. The **Republicans** admired Grant's work. So, in 1868, they chose him to run for president. Grant easily won the election.

★ DID YOU KNOW? ★

The salary of the president doubled from $25,000 to $50,000 during Grant's time in office.

General Lee and General Grant met
at the McLean House in Virginia to discuss
the terms of surrender.

President Grant

Grant took office on March 4, 1869. He was just 46 years old. At the time, he was the youngest president in US history.

As president, Grant worked with Congress to pass the Fifteenth **Amendment**. This law gave African-American men the right to vote. However, many Americans did not agree with the law.

SUPREME COURT ★ APPOINTMENTS

William Strong: 1870

Joseph P. Bradley: 1870

Ward Hunt: 1873

Morrison Remick Waite: 1874

Congress passed the Fifteenth Amendment in 1869. It became law on March 30, 1870.

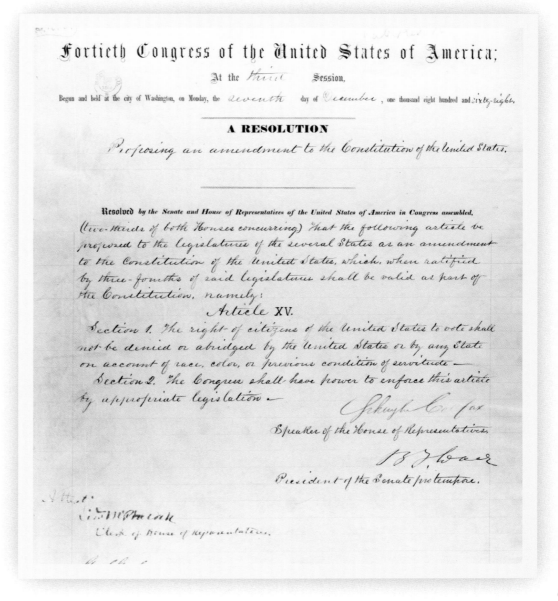

Some Southerners actually tried to keep African-American men from voting. So, Grant signed four Force Acts. These laws secured the voting rights of African Americans.

Grant was reelected in 1872. He faced **challenges** in his second term. Many people he trusted took part in **scandals**. Because of this, many Americans thought less of Grant.

Then, in 1873, a national financial panic occurred. Many people wanted Congress to print more **greenbacks**. However, greenbacks were not backed by gold. Grant believed printing more of them would hurt the **economy**. So, he **vetoed** Congress's bill.

PRESIDENT GRANT'S CABINET

First Term
March 4, 1869–March 4, 1873

★ **STATE:** Elihu B. Washburne,
Hamilton Fish (from March 17, 1869)

★ **TREASURY:** George S. Boutwell

★ **WAR:** John A. Rawlins,
William T. Sherman (from September 11, 1869),
William W. Belknap (from November 1, 1869)

★ **NAVY:** Adolph E. Borie,
George M. Robeson (from June 25, 1869)

★ **ATTORNEY GENERAL:** Ebenezer R. Hoar,
Amos T. Akerman (from July 8, 1870),
George H. Williams (from January 10, 1872)

★ **INTERIOR:** Jacob D. Cox,
Columbus Delano (from November 1, 1870)

Second Term
March 4, 1873–March 4, 1877

★ **STATE:** Hamilton Fish

★ **TREASURY:** William A. Richardson,
Benjamin H. Bristow (from June 4, 1874),
Lot M. Morrill (from July 7, 1876)

★ **WAR:** William W. Belknap,
Alphonso Taft (from March 11, 1876),
James D. Cameron (from June 1, 1876)

★ **NAVY:** George M. Robeson

★ **ATTORNEY GENERAL:** George H. Williams,
Edward Pierrepont (from May 15, 1875),
Alphonso Taft (from June 1, 1876)

★ **INTERIOR:** Columbus Delano,
Zachariah Chandler (from October 19, 1875)

Around the World

Some **Republicans** wanted Grant to run for a third term. But, he did not want to be president again. Grant left the White House in March 1877.

In May, the Grants left for a trip around the world. Everywhere they went, people cheered. They called Grant the leader who kept America together.

After two years, the Grants returned to the United States. The family had little money left after their travels. They soon went broke.

The Grants visited many countries in Europe. They also went to Africa, the Middle East, India, and Asia.

In 1884, Grant found out he had throat **cancer**. He wanted his family to have enough money after he died. So, he wrote a book about his life.

Ulysses S. Grant died on July 23, 1885. The nation was saddened by his death. Grant was buried in New York, overlooking the Hudson River.

Grant's book came out after his death. It made enough money to provide for his family for the rest of their lives. Ulysses S. Grant had a **challenging** presidency. Yet, he remains one of the nation's greatest military heroes.

In 1959, Grant's burial site became a national memorial.

Office of the President

Branches of Government

The US government has three branches. They are the executive, legislative, and judicial branches. Each branch has some power over the others. This is called a system of checks and balances.

★ Executive Branch

The executive branch enforces laws. It is made up of the president, the vice president, and the president's cabinet. The president represents the United States around the world. He or she also signs bills into law and leads the military.

★ Legislative Branch

The legislative branch makes laws, maintains the military, and regulates trade. It also has the power to declare war. This branch includes the Senate and the House of Representatives. Together, these two houses form Congress.

★ Judicial Branch

The judicial branch interprets laws. It is made up of district courts, courts of appeals, and the Supreme Court. District courts try cases. Sometimes people disagree with a trial's outcome. Then he or she may appeal. If a court of appeals supports the ruling, a person may appeal to the Supreme Court.

Qualifications for Office

To be president, a candidate must be at least 35 years old. The person must be a natural-born US citizen. He or she must also have lived in the United States for at least 14 years.

Electoral College

The US presidential election is an indirect election. Voters from each state choose electors. These electors represent their state in the Electoral College. Each elector has one electoral vote. Electors cast their vote for the candidate with the highest number of votes from people in their state. A candidate must receive the majority of Electoral College votes to win.

Term of Office

Each president may be elected to two four-year terms. The presidential election is held on the Tuesday after the first Monday in November. The president is sworn in on January 20 of the following year. At that time, he or she takes the oath of office.
It states:

> I do solemnly swear (or affirm) that I will faithfully execute the office of President of the United States, and will to the best of my ability, preserve, protect and defend the Constitution of the United States.

Line of Succession

The Presidential Succession Act of 1947 states who becomes president if the president cannot serve. The vice president is first in the line. Next are the Speaker of the House and the President Pro Tempore of the Senate. It may happen that none of these individuals is able to serve. Then the office falls to the president's cabinet members. They would take office in the order in which each department was created:

Secretary of State

Secretary of the Treasury

Secretary of Defense

Attorney General

Secretary of the Interior

Secretary of Agriculture

Secretary of Commerce

Secretary of Labor

Secretary of Health and Human Services

Secretary of Housing and Urban Development

Secretary of Transportation

Secretary of Energy

Secretary of Education

Secretary of Veterans Affairs

Secretary of Homeland Security

Benefits

★ While in office, the president receives a salary. It is $400,000 per year. He or she lives in the White House. The president also has 24-hour Secret Service protection.

★ The president may travel on a Boeing 747 jet. This special jet is called Air Force One. It can hold 70 passengers. It has kitchens, a dining room, sleeping areas, and more. Air Force One can fly halfway around the world before needing to refuel. It can even refuel in flight!

★ When the president travels by car, he or she uses Cadillac One. It is a Cadillac Deville that has been modified. The car has heavy armor and communications systems. The president may even take Cadillac One along when visiting other countries.

★ The president also travels on a helicopter. It is called Marine One. It may also be taken along when the president visits other countries.

★ Sometimes the president needs to get away with family and friends. Camp David is the official presidential retreat. It is located in Maryland. The US Navy maintains the retreat. The US Marine Corps keeps it secure. The camp offers swimming, tennis, golf, and hiking.

★ When the president leaves office, he or she receives lifetime Secret Service protection. He or she also receives a yearly pension of $203,700. The former president also receives money for office space, supplies, and staff.

33

PRESIDENTS AND THEIR TERMS

PRESIDENT	PARTY	TOOK OFFICE	LEFT OFFICE	TERMS SERVED	VICE PRESIDENT
George Washington	None	April 30, 1789	March 4, 1797	Two	John Adams
John Adams	Federalist	March 4, 1797	March 4, 1801	One	Thomas Jefferson
Thomas Jefferson	Democratic-Republican	March 4, 1801	March 4, 1809	Two	Aaron Burr, George Clinton
James Madison	Democratic-Republican	March 4, 1809	March 4, 1817	Two	George Clinton, Elbridge Gerry
James Monroe	Democratic-Republican	March 4, 1817	March 4, 1825	Two	Daniel D. Tompkins
John Quincy Adams	Democratic-Republican	March 4, 1825	March 4, 1829	One	John C. Calhoun
Andrew Jackson	Democrat	March 4, 1829	March 4, 1837	Two	John C. Calhoun, Martin Van Buren
Martin Van Buren	Democrat	March 4, 1837	March 4, 1841	One	Richard M. Johnson
William H. Harrison	Whig	March 4, 1841	April 4, 1841	Died During First Term	John Tyler
John Tyler	Whig	April 6, 1841	March 4, 1845	Completed Harrison's Term	Office Vacant
James K. Polk	Democrat	March 4, 1845	March 4, 1849	One	George M. Dallas
Zachary Taylor	Whig	March 5, 1849	July 9, 1850	Died During First Term	Millard Fillmore

PRESIDENT	PARTY	TOOK OFFICE	LEFT OFFICE	TERMS SERVED	VICE PRESIDENT
Millard Fillmore	Whig	July 10, 1850	March 4, 1853	Completed Taylor's Term	Office Vacant
Franklin Pierce	Democrat	March 4, 1853	March 4, 1857	One	William R.D. King
James Buchanan	Democrat	March 4, 1857	March 4, 1861	One	John C. Breckinridge
Abraham Lincoln	Republican	March 4, 1861	April 15, 1865	Served One Term, Died During Second Term	Hannibal Hamlin, Andrew Johnson
Andrew Johnson	Democrat	April 15, 1865	March 4, 1869	Completed Lincoln's Second Term	Office Vacant
Ulysses S. Grant	Republican	March 4, 1869	March 4, 1877	Two	Schuyler Colfax, Henry Wilson
Rutherford B. Hayes	Republican	March 3, 1877	March 4, 1881	One	William A. Wheeler
James A. Garfield	Republican	March 4, 1881	September 19, 1881	Died During First Term	Chester Arthur
Chester Arthur	Republican	September 20, 1881	March 4, 1885	Completed Garfield's Term	Office Vacant
Grover Cleveland	Democrat	March 4, 1885	March 4, 1889	One	Thomas A. Hendricks
Benjamin Harrison	Republican	March 4, 1889	March 4, 1893	One	Levi P. Morton
Grover Cleveland	Democrat	March 4, 1893	March 4, 1897	One	Adlai E. Stevenson
William McKinley	Republican	March 4, 1897	September 14, 1901	Served One Term, Died During Second Term	Garret A. Hobart, Theodore Roosevelt

PRESIDENT	PARTY	TOOK OFFICE	LEFT OFFICE	TERMS SERVED	VICE PRESIDENT
Theodore Roosevelt	Republican	September 14, 1901	March 4, 1909	Completed McKinley's Second Term, Served One Term	Office Vacant, Charles Fairbanks
William Taft	Republican	March 4, 1909	March 4, 1913	One	James S. Sherman
Woodrow Wilson	Democrat	March 4, 1913	March 4, 1921	Two	Thomas R. Marshall
Warren G. Harding	Republican	March 4, 1921	August 2, 1923	Died During First Term	Calvin Coolidge
Calvin Coolidge	Republican	August 3, 1923	March 4, 1929	Completed Harding's Term, Served One Term	Office Vacant, Charles Dawes
Herbert Hoover	Republican	March 4, 1929	March 4, 1933	One	Charles Curtis
Franklin D. Roosevelt	Democrat	March 4, 1933	April 12, 1945	Served Three Terms, Died During Fourth Term	John Nance Garner, Henry A. Wallace, Harry S. Truman
Harry S. Truman	Democrat	April 12, 1945	January 20, 1953	Completed Roosevelt's Fourth Term, Served One Term	Office Vacant, Alben Barkley
Dwight D. Eisenhower	Republican	January 20, 1953	January 20, 1961	Two	Richard Nixon
John F. Kennedy	Democrat	January 20, 1961	November 22, 1963	Died During First Term	Lyndon B. Johnson
Lyndon B. Johnson	Democrat	November 22, 1963	January 20, 1969	Completed Kennedy's Term, Served One Term	Office Vacant, Hubert H. Humphrey
Richard Nixon	Republican	January 20, 1969	August 9, 1974	Completed First Term, Resigned During Second Term	Spiro T. Agnew, Gerald Ford

PRESIDENT	PARTY	TOOK OFFICE	LEFT OFFICE	TERMS SERVED	VICE PRESIDENT
Gerald Ford	Republican	August 9, 1974	January 20, 1977	Completed Nixon's Second Term	Nelson A. Rockefeller
Jimmy Carter	Democrat	January 20, 1977	January 20, 1981	One	Walter Mondale
Ronald Reagan	Republican	January 20, 1981	January 20, 1989	Two	George H.W. Bush
George H.W. Bush	Republican	January 20, 1989	January 20, 1993	One	Dan Quayle
Bill Clinton	Democrat	January 20, 1993	January 20, 2001	Two	Al Gore
George W. Bush	Republican	January 20, 2001	January 20, 2009	Two	Dick Cheney
Barack Obama	Democrat	January 20, 2009	January 20, 2017	Two	Joe Biden

"Let us have peace." Ulysses S. Grant

★ WRITE TO THE PRESIDENT ★

You may write to the president at:
The White House
1600 Pennsylvania Avenue NW
Washington, DC 20500

You may e-mail the president at:
comments@whitehouse.gov

37

Glossary

academy—a private school that trains students in a certain field.

amendment—a change to a country's or a state's constitution.

American Civil War—the war between the Northern and Southern states from 1861 to 1865.

annex—to take land and add it to a nation.

brevet—a military title given to an officer who has a higher rank than he or she is paid for.

cancer—any of a group of very harmful diseases that cause a body's cells to become unhealthy.

challenge (CHA-luhnj)—something that tests one's strengths or abilities.

Confederate States of America—the group of 11 Southern states that declared independence during the American Civil War. It is also called the Confederacy.

economy—the way that a country produces, sells, and buys goods and services.

greenback—paper money printed during the American Civil War.

Mexican-American War—a war between the United States and Mexico that lasted from 1846 to 1848.

real estate—the business of selling buildings and land.

Republican—a member of the Republican political party.

reputation—a person's quality of character, as judged by other people.

scandal—an action that shocks people and disgraces those connected with it.

secretary of war—a member of the president's cabinet who handled the military and national defense.

surrender—to give up.

Union—the Northern states that remained part of the United States during the American Civil War.

veto—the right of one member of a decision-making group to stop an action by the group. In the US government, the president can veto bills passed by Congress. But Congress can override the president's veto if two-thirds of its members vote to do so.

★ WEBSITES ★

To learn more about the US Presidents, visit **booklinks.abdopublishing.com**. These links are routinely monitored and updated to provide the most current information available.

Index

American Civil War   **6, 7, 16, 17, 18, 19, 20, 21**

birth   **6, 8**

book   **28**

childhood   **8**

civil rights   **22, 23, 24**

death   **7, 8, 28, 29**

education   **6, 8, 10, 11**

family   **8, 10, 12, 14, 15, 26, 27, 28**

farming   **8, 14**

Fifteenth Amendment   **4, 22, 23**

financial panic   **24**

Force Acts   **24**

Johnson, Andrew   **20**

leather shop   **14**

Lee, Robert E.   **20, 21**

Mexican-American War   **12, 13, 14**

military service   **4, 6, 10, 12, 13, 14, 16, 17, 18, 19, 20, 21, 28**

real estate   **14**

Republican Party   **8, 20, 26**

scandals   **4, 24**

secretary of war   **20**

slavery   **16**

world travel   **26, 27**